Getting Naked
to
Get Free

Getting Naked
to
Get Free

J. FREDERIKA

iUniverse®

GETTING NAKED TO GET FREE

iUniverse books may be ordered through booksellers or by contacting:

iUniverse
1663 Liberty Drive
Bloomington, IN 47403
www.iuniverse.com
1-800-Authors (1-800-288-4677)

Because of the dynamic nature of the Internet, any web addresses or links contained in this book may have changed since publication and may no longer be valid. The views expressed in this work are solely those of the author and do not necessarily reflect the views of the publisher, and the publisher hereby disclaims any responsibility for them.

Any people depicted in stock imagery provided by Thinkstock are models, and such images are being used for illustrative purposes only.
Certain stock imagery © Thinkstock.

ISBN: 978-1-4917-9020-5 (sc)
ISBN: 978-1-4917-9019-9 (e)

Library of Congress Control Number: 2016903043

Print information available on the last page.

iUniverse rev. date: 03/08/2016

Pauline and Alberta, I hope you are proud.

Contents

Acknowledgments

I am thankful for the many ways that God has graced us to do the work of healing in our communities. Among those doing the work are activists, organizers, protestors, preachers, and poets. I know so many wonderful people who are doing the work of liberation and healing who challenge me to answer the call, daily. And I hope, in some small way, to make a contribution to that work.

I want to thank my mom and my brother for listening to me talk about my dreams and for encouraging me to write, no matter how much I bored them. I know that over the past three years, some of my behavior has been uncharacteristic and perhaps even a bit strange. I've walked away from what many believed was a good career in order to finish school and pursue my dreams. I've committed all of my time, outside of my studies to the work of I Just Believe Ministries because I believe in creating safe spaces for women to heal. And you celebrated me throughout the process, and I love you.

Thank you to my family and friends for all their love and support. I also want to thank my mentors and teachers, especially Dr. McMillan, Dr. Bridgeman and Dr. Kinney for pushing me to rediscover my voice and to fully embrace how God is working through me. Thank you to my classmates and professors for their constant encouragement and for challenging me to grow and share. You will never know what your love and support means to me. I am truly grateful to call you friend.

Thank you to For Harriet for publishing earlier versions of "Sleep without Sleeping" and "Righteous Rage." I was encouraged by your feedback. And thank you to the DC Poetry Project, Inc. for the working sessions, open mic and critique. I am grateful for the platform.

And lastly, I want to thank you, the reader. This journey for me began a few years ago. And every time I picked up a pen, I thought about you. I thought about sexual abuse and domestic violence survivors. I thought about families impacted by mental illness and suicide. I thought about people who have pressed and continue to press their way through very painful circumstances. I wanted to be one of the voices reminding you that you are not alone. Thank you for pressing and thank you for allowing me to share this truth with you.

Introduction

On August 29, 2013, I was sitting on my sofa, replaying a news report I had seen that morning. A man accused of raping a fourteen-year-old girl was sentenced to thirty days in prison. The judge commented that the young lady seemed far older than her chronological age which played a part in the sentencing. I was incensed, especially after hearing that she later died by suicide. I began to think about the countless girls that are discounted even after they tell their story. I thought about the women who carry the shame of abuse and remain silent.

So I sat, cried and yelled and cried some more. And at 7:52 I began to write. By 8:12 I had finished the poem "Sleep without Sleeping." I walked around my apartment all night, reciting the work. I even sent it in an e-mail to friends. With every word, I came alive. I couldn't believe it. I felt alive—more alive than I had felt in quite some time.

The truth is that I had been stuck for a long time. I was unhappy at work, in church, and at home. Something was missing. And I realized, after writing that first piece, that it was me that was missing. And I wanted me back.

Thinking back on my childhood dreams, I wanted to be an activist, an author, and a motivational speaker. I made a commitment to myself when I was fifteen that I would work with women who had been abused, but I had not been true to my pledge. Yes, I facilitated workshops on sexual-abuse awareness and worked with survivors of domestic violence. But I was not honoring the commitment, not by a long shot. And I realized I hadn't honored the promise, because I was still stuck in my shame. In order to really do the work, I would have to stop hiding. I think I was hiding because part of me believed that if people really knew me that I would be disqualified. I shared my story before, but it was sanitized so that others wouldn't be offended. It was contained so that I could show that I had it all together. But the truth is that I still needed help. Going through this process, I fully embraced these facts: I am not what has happened to me and I am enough.

Accepting that I am enough meant that I had to get naked. Getting naked meant that I had to acknowledge and share some things about my life that I kept hidden for a long time. Getting naked meant that I'd have to have difficult conversations with family. Getting naked meant that I would have to really examine the impact that sexual abuse had and was still having on my life. Sometimes just being able to speak your truth can be a life altering event. It was during this season that I rediscovered and fully embraced my voice and my purpose.

The poems you'll read over the next several pages are very personal, as they deal with sexual abuse, domestic violence, mental illness, and other things no one ever talked about while I was growing up. Some of the pieces are my truth. Some of the pieces you might find true for you. They are the secrets that everyone in the family knows, but won't necessarily acknowledge. They are the pain with which many live because they are unable to find relief.

Reading the poems may trigger sadness or anger for you and if that happens, put the book down for a minute. I know it can be hard to do alone, so find a safe space and a good friend. Heck, get a journal and a good therapist too. Whatever you do, I want you to know that you do not have to go through it alone.

My prayer is that you will read this raw and vulnerable account of a young woman's life and find ways create opportunities to help other women to share their truth in a healing and safe environment. Perhaps, as you read Sleep Without Sleeping, you will give thought to what you, your organization or congregation might do to address sexual abuse and assault and to minister to survivors. Perhaps as you read, Escape, you will consider how you can support and minister to families impacted by mental illness and suicide.

Shame has a way of silencing us; holding us hostage. But people are hurting. And we cannot continue to suggest that they swallow up their pain, forget their story and move on. God requires more of us. We must be agents of healing. We must create safe spaces for healing. Let's tell our stories! Let's get naked so we can get free!

0

August is better than September,
So I'm coming early.
I'm not sure my folks are ready.
I'm not sure I'm ready.
I don't know what this journey will bring.

Boot Camp

I once read that incest is boot camp for prostitution,
and I got enrolled at age six.
I didn't know it at the time,
but he was grooming me for that life,
that existence where I don't belong to me,
where I am nothing more than an object used for sick people's satisfaction,
where I am invisible,
except for the holes I possess that stretch open wide enough to fit a penis.

I was a kid,
forcefully being groomed for that life.
I didn't sign up for this,
yet I can't seem to escape it,
and the training is rigorous.

There's no cardio,
just conditioning to keep silent.
There's no push-ups,
just teachings not to push back.
There's no weight lifting,
just training to carry the weight of guilt and shame.

I once tried to run away,
but he found me,
beat me,
raped me,
and beat me again.
So as much as I want to leave,
I can't get out of it.

And I know when you see me,
you immediately think,
Prostitute turning tricks.

But you don't know my story.
I was groomed for this.
Hell, I've been training since I was six.

Dirty Nails
(A Haiku)

Plucked her virtue and
planted shame. She's still trying,
to pull up the weeds.

6

I divide my time
between Mommy and Daddy.
I haven't figured out
if I am supposed to divide my love,
the way they divided their belongings.
I'm learning to live in two worlds.
Some might call it fractured,
But there are no How-To books for me.
And no one talks to a six-year-old about divorce.

Sleep without Sleeping

I never did tell anyone about the times he touched me when I was six.
It's probably because I didn't say stop.
I didn't know I should.
I didn't know I could.
After all he was family.

The painful urination eventually stopped,
and I came to expect him—
finger,
penis,
and tongue.

I learned how to sleep without sleeping,
always aware of every movement around me.

That sound is my baby brother leaving his room to go to the bathroom.
And that sound is my mom,
going downstairs now, no doubt for a Pepsi and some pretzels.
She always wanted a Pepsi and some pretzels.

And that sound is him,
using the connecting door to enter my room
once he thinks everyone is asleep.

But I learned to sleep without sleeping,
to always be aware of every movement around me.
And I know he's coming.

Even before he enters the room,
I can hear him.
Even before he is close to me,
I can smell him.
Even before he touches me,
I can taste his breath.

He stopped once I was ten,
and I didn't see him after that for almost ten years.
I no longer had to pretend to sleep,
but I had learned to sleep without sleeping,
to always be aware of every movement around me.
Yet I was completely oblivious to what was happening in me.

Because of what he did to me,
in me, grew shame, anger, and disgust.
And those deadly seeds, once planted,
would take years to pluck up.
Always trying to fill that void,
I went looking for love in all the wrong places.
I was stuck. .

I was pregnant at thirteen,
yet no one ever checked to see if anything had ever happened to me.
They just assumed it was me.

"Fast" was what my mom called it,
what she called me.
Why would she assume it was me?
I hated her for that.

I thought for a while that she hated me too.
So I learned how to be with her—
I mean, live with her while being apart—
connected by DNA but disconnected at heart.

It took years for me to like her,
to not hold what he did to me against her.
Then at fifteen I had an epiphany.
In order to be free,
I could no longer let my mother's disappointment have power over me.

When I saw him again,
it was at my grandmother's funeral.
I was nineteen by then.
Someone there told me he lived in a shelter when he was a kid and was
probably abused.
It's no excuse for what he did,
but holding on to it the way I did was choking the life out of me.

And again I had an epiphany.
In order to be free,
I had to take back my cousin's power over me.
And I did.

But the hardest work was learning to like me,
not hold what he did to me against me,
not let what he did to me define me.

I didn't realize it until now,
but I hadn't dealt with me.
I had pardoned everyone else but me.

Damn!
I never even allowed myself to cry,
to really feel the hurt, anger, or pain.

I left that me in Philly with all her bitterness and rage.
Until one day the me I buried was resurrected from her grave
and forced me back to me to deal with all the anger and shame.

Then one night in August,
I sat with my tears, anger, and hurt.
I gathered my strength
and took a deep breath.

I told that six-year-old, "It wasn't your fault."
I told that thirteen-year-old, "You shouldn't have had to go to the clinic
alone."
I told that twenty-year-old, "You are special just the way you are."
I told that twenty-seven-year old, "You don't have to hide who you are.
You just have to be the best you."
I told that thirty-year-old, "You've come a long way but still have work
to do."
I told that thirty-five-year-old, "It is okay to smile and cry because it
doesn't say you're weak."
I told that thirty-six-year-old, "Get yourself some sleep."
Because I had learned to sleep without sleeping,
to always be aware of every movement around me.
And at thirty-six,
it was becoming tiring.

So for the first time in a long while I slept.
And it wasn't the sleep without sleeping I had become accustomed to doing for thirty years.
I really slept
without waiting for the connecting door to open.
I slept
without hearing or smelling him or tasting his breath.
I slept
without pretending not to notice the unwanted finger, penis, or tongue.
I slept
for the first time in a long time.
I was finally able to sleep.

Because At thirty-six I had another epiphany.
In order to really be free,
I couldn't hold my past against me.

Predators
(A Haiku)

Incest was boot camp.
Prostitution was just work.
He groomed her for this.

Summer Used to Be My Friend

There's a lull in the middle of the night.
Everything's dark—
no yelling,
punching,
or crying.
No one is begging for him to stop.
No sons are sitting in the corner with covered ears and tears streaming
down their faces.
No daughters are plotting revenge.
There's just silence.

I should be asleep,
yet I'm still wide awake,
replaying the noises of the day,
rehearsing how I'll fight if he ever comes for me that way,
and wondering why no one says anything.

Looking toward the window,
I notice day attempting to break through.
Soon everyone will be awake,
pretending not to notice the bruises he left
or the screams heard the night before.

We will walk on eggshells,
wear our best fake smiles,
and pretend that all is well.

We've been taught to ignore our pain,
even if it kills us.
I'm only here for the summer.
So as soon as this summer ends,
things can go back to normal.
I won't have to pretend I don't hear the screams for help,
see her purplish-black eye,
or notice my brothers growing bitter inside
as they watch their mother's spirit die.

But I fear that it will be hard to return to normal.
I've witnessed so many beatings,
that the sight of abuse no longer makes me ill.
I fear that I'll be her twenty years from now.
That thought gives me chills.

When fall is here,
I cannot unsee the bruises.
In winter and spring,
I can still hear the screams.
I carry the pain of summer with me long after the season ends.
And before you know it,
it's time to go back and pretend.
To think summer used to be my friend.

What the Sitter Said
(A Haiku)

Just relax, baby.
Promise I'm a good teacher.
Shhhh! Put your hand here.

11

I built up the courage
to tell him not to touch me.
And he stopped
for good.
Sometimes I wonder,
Did he moved on to someone else?

Like Them

She could see the anger in his eyes.
He wanted to hit her like he did his other women.
So she wasn't surprised when his fist connected with her jaw.
But she was his daughter.
She was not like them.
And she was not afraid.

He grabbed her by her hair
and shoved her around.
But she refused to shed a tear.
Even after being thrown to the ground,
she refused to shed a tear.
She would not let him beat fear into her.
She was his daughter.
She was not like them.
And she was not afraid.

In between the smacks and the punches,
she raised her voice
and said, "You know this is wrong, don't you?"
She doesn't even think he heard her.
She tried to catch his fist with her hand.
But he was too strong.
So she kicked and attempted to run upstairs.
He grabbed her foot,
pulled her down to the first step,
and ended the beating with this threat,
"You aren't going home. You'll live here with me instead."

He raised his fist once more,
and she could hear his wife scream from a distance,
"Stop! You're hurting her!"

But she told her not to worry.
She wouldn't let him do to her
what he had done to so many others.
You see,
worse than their black eyes and busted lips,
he had crushed their esteem with his words.
He had wounded their spirits with his fist.
She would not let him do that to her.

She was not like them.
She was his daughter.
And she was not afraid.

But after that night,
she said nothing.
Just like everyone else,
she stayed silent,
so maybe—
just maybe—
she was just like them.

It's 1988

The first Monday of summer break,
I ditched the sweater dresses for tank tops and jean shorts.
I made my way outside early.
With jump rope in one hand and radio in the other,
I played Al B. Sure's "Night and Day."
Friends joined in singing loudly.
We played Public Enemy and N.W.A
with the volume low since Mom thinks I already threw those tapes away.
She did tell me to do that,
but I never listened.
We played "A Salt with a Deadly Pepa" and worked on our dance routines,
trying to be seen.

We saw the new boys across the street.
They said they were visiting their cousin.
I picked out the one I wanted
since they were gonna be here the whole summer.
He had a Gumby and beautiful smile.
He would be mine before the summer was over.
His smile was silent recognition that he wanted me too.

I wrote in my diary about the love I hoped to find
one day
soon.
This summer was gonna be great.

The Cycle Continues
(It's 1989)

His beautiful eyes invite me to love.
His voice, so smooth, is like music to my ears.
His arms are wrapped 'round me tightly like a glove.
His presence tells me there's nothing to fear.
So I commit to give him all of me,
without hesitation,
fear,
or regret.
And he loved me ever so gently.

I hoped this was a glimpse of how good love would get.
That lovin' was good.
In fact it was great,
every kiss and touch,
each and every time.
I did whatever he asked with no debate,
simply because I believed he was mine.

Days have now passed,
and he hasn't returned.
I'm heartbroken again.
Will I ever learn?

Point of No Return

She hears her name,
a reminder that there is no turning back.
And she's starting to think maybe they were right about her.

She moves quickly to the room
while everything else seems to be moving in slow motion.

Gets in position.

Is that an IV? She wonders.
It is.
How do they expect her to keep her arm straight?
How long will this be?
She thinks,
You don't deserve to be in a comfortable position.
So she won't let them put her to sleep.

IV in arm,
but she is determined to be strong, all the way through.
She wonders
Twenty years from now …
Will people be able to look at me and see what I've done?
Will they treat me differently if they knew?
Will I ever be the same?

Before she is able to answer,
they move her to the recovery room.
She doesn't know it now,
but soon she'll realize
that no one ever recovers in that room.
Recovery comes over time.

After

For months, heard sounds like
a garbage disposal,
ringing her my ear.
Doctor said it was nothing wrong,
at least not with my hearing.
I guess he wasn't trained to diagnose shame.

15

I stand alone,
stuck in my shame,
unable to find words for my pain.
When no one sees me,
I let my tears water my wounds.

Love Hurts

Despite the punches,
I stay.
Just a black eye and busted lip,
it's not bad.
I've had worse.

That Night on Campus
(1995)

Before you hear my story,
you will have already determined
whether I am worthy of your sympathy.
You'll want to know what I was wearing,
what I said,
or if I had anything to drink.

You'll want to know if I smiled.
Did I flirt?
Why did I go to the party in the first place?
Your micro-aggressions will sound like questions,
so you don't have to say the words, "You asked for it."

You'll critique my coming forward as another conspiracy against the black man.
For proof, you'll require pictures of him on top of me
and voice recordings of me saying no ...
screaming no.
You'll need to see the tears,
cuts,
blood,
and vaginal bruising,
all as a sign of my truth.

You will send me interesting articles
about how to walk in pairs while on campus
and reminders to park my car where there is ample lighting.

You will offer self-defense classes,
so I can learn how to fight back the next time I'm attacked,
almost as if you know there will be a next time.

You'll convene an assembly
and inform the students about violence on campus.
You'll remind the women to be extra vigilant and to dress with class,
nothing low-cut and nothing too short.

We all know there is proof
that women who cover themselves respect themselves,
and women who respect themselves force others to respect them,
thus eliminating them from the pool of women who deserve to be raped.

I, on the other hand, chose to wear those tight jeans and formfitting
V-neck sweater.
You will get angry
when I question why you prefer to regulate my dress
rather than police your sons' behavior.
You will be incensed
when I suggest that you prefer to control my wine intake
rather than talk to your sons about rape.

You will sit in silence
when I ask you what you will say to your daughters.

I Deserve It

Yeah, my man hits me.
I guess I deserve it.
He likes his dinner ready by six.
He wants it hot and won't settle for less.

So if it isn't ready by six,
I deserve to be hit.
The bruises go away eventually.
It's not that deep.
I'm not being whipped.
Hell, it's just a black eye,
maybe a busted lip.

Oh, one time he broke my jaw.
But that's because I let my tongue slip.
But, you see, it doesn't happen often.
And I know, when it does, he's really sorry.

But it's my fault.
I shouldn't have made him so mad.
I know he really loves me.
So when I make him angry,
don't do what I'm told,
knowing he will be pissed,
it's his place to set me straight,
even if he does it with his fist.

My Day in Reverse

I spit the bullet back into the gun,
lower my hand,
and place it back on the table.

No longer seated,
I shuffle backward up the stairs into the room.
Standing side by side now,
I unwrap my fingers from around your neck
as we tussle backward toward the bed.
With me on top,
I swallow up the obscenities I screamed.

The blood on your shirt returns to your lip,
as my fist disconnects from your jaw.

You suck up your screams
as your hair breaks free from the grip of my fingers.
You are back in the bathroom.
You are standing at the mirror,
putting on that red lipstick.

As I stand at the door of the master bath.
You ask,
"Honey, where were you today?"

Tonight

Instead of confronting my pain,
I find another way to make it from day to day.
On most days it leaves me numb.
And some days I barely have enough strength to raise my kids.
They see my pain.
But their little brains have yet to develop the vocabulary needed to articulate their concern.
So they say nothing except
Mommy, I love you …
Mommy, I'm hungry …
Mommy, I'm sleepy.

But I don't hear them over the voice in my own head,
telling me I'm worthless.
Reaching for the syringe,
I'm thinkin', *Nothing else has taken the pain away.*
Maybe this heroin will.

Depression

I once heard someone say that a depressed Christian is a contradiction.
Yet day after day, I awaken,
hoping today I feel alive enough to smile
instead of lingering in this place
where others often mistake
the darkness through which I attempt to navigate as a lack of faith.

I love God,
yet this overwhelming sadness I cannot escape.
Maybe I need medication,
because I can't pray it away.

Floating

Yesterday I smoked away the last my dreams,
accepted my painful reality,
and dismissed any possibility
for healing.

Completely detached from me,
I became numb at the thought of what I should have been.

But please don't show me any pity.
I chose this life.
Well, maybe this life chose me.'
Early.

I mean,
early like Mighty Mouse on Saturday mornings,
early like someone should have noticed the warning signs,
early like Unc asking to borrow five dollars as soon as I arrive at Grandma's
house.

I learned early how to hide my money in a Crown Royal bag,
I learned early how to keep my valuables away from people with shifty hands,
most valuables that is.
I learned early how to shoot craps and play tonk.
I learned early how to drink with the big dogs without getting drunk.
I learned early how to light that pipe and take a long puff.
I learned early how to escape whenever I want.

So yesterday I smoked away the last of my dreams.
It's too difficult staying clean
when for so long I've been bleeding.
My family throws me Band-Aids,
hoping I'll disappear without a trace
so they don't have to explain to outsiders why I stink.

But you'd stink too if your cuts were never cleansed
and your wounds had never healed.
Pain like pus oozes from my spirit.
Injuries scream,
but nobody hears.

So I'm just gonna sit here and fade away.
Won't nobody miss me no way.

Suicide

I'm sitting here,
somewhere between earth and heaven,
hoping to God that someone notices me
floating away.

Escape

They found you in the car.
I cannot imagine how they felt at that moment,
maybe like losing one's soul yet still alive,
like being somewhere between unable to breathe and unable to die,
wondering why.

The heart silently pleads why,
but there's no strength to actually scream, "Why?"
Can somebody just tell me why?
Why is this happening to us?

I imagine you,
gun in hand,
determined this time.
You have no strength left to fight,
or maybe you're full of strength,
enough to say, "This is enough."

You sit,
acknowledging there are things worse than death.
With your finger on the trigger,
you don't pause to consider what happens after.
There's no thought to the impact of the absence of your laughter.

No hot thread carved through the wind.
No spiraling bullet ...
no spin ...
no space between metal and skin.

It's just metal on skin,
your skin
now broken open,
wide enough for you to escape.

Present

Can I just sit with you for a while?
We don't have to speak.
We can just sit in silence,
and I can hold your hand or not.
Or you can rest your head on my shoulder or not,
and you can yell,
cry,
or cuss.

I promise not to tell you how I know things will be better tomorrow.
Because the truth is,
I don't know.
And I know how upset that makes you.
If you want,
we can sit and stare at the ceiling
or the night's sky.
We can drink a glass of wine,
play some music,
or do whatever you need,
if it's what you need
in this moment
so you can make it to the next moment.
I'm here.

21

I used to call my lover by the wrong name.
He loved me anyway.
Until one day, he didn't.
Sometimes I miss him.

Lonely

She wore high heels and red lipstick.
She laughed out loud without apology.
She liked jazz and slow jams.
She would guide a man's hands to her hips
and sway from side to side while she danced.
She was known to sing in her lover's ear.
And her kiss would make any man wanna buy what she was selling.

She spoke in a whisper.
Her words would capture her lover's heart,
which was now in her hand.
After playing his heart,
she would place it on the shelf next to her own.
She could never give it away,
She preferred to hold on to theirs instead.

It never worked.
So I—
I mean, she—
would eventually
return their hearts to them,
now battered and bruised.
She couldn't care for theirs
until mine—
I mean, hers—
had healed.

And when no one is looking,
I—
I mean, she—
comforts herself with her music and her tears,
knowing that her lovers could only provide temporary relief
for the pain and grief she's accumulated over the years.

Her fear is that one day she'll wake up with
no jazz or slow jams,
no lover's hands on her hips,
no hearts on the shelf,
no one to kiss,
and no ears to catch her whisper.

Just my—
I mean, just her—
red lipstick and high heels
laughing out loud
without apology
alone.

Jealousy

No singing
No dancing
I've lost all sense of rhythm
Just knowing your sweet music
Is playing for her.

27

I learned to wear this mask in church.
They told me the truth would set me free.
But I saw them cringe
when I shared my truth.
It let me know that they'd prefer
a more sanitized version of my testimony.

So I wore the mask.
Until I realized that by hiding from my truth,
I could never be me.

Him

When we were together,
you broke my heart.
I stay far away from love now.

I realize that it wasn't your fault.
But you could have found the words to say,
"I'm not ready for this".

You were the only person I ever allowed to see me.
I mean really see me,
all of me.

For you, I tore down walls
that took years to construct.
I was open, vulnerable.

Now I wish I could forget
the feel of your lips,
the look in your eyes,
your laugh.
Those plans we made,
together,
are still posted on my wall,
waiting to be fulfilled.

Sometimes I Cry

I refuse to censor my tears
because they make you feel uncomfortable.
They are mine.
My tears speak a language that the Almighty understands.
And God carefully bottles each one,
keeping track, I suppose.
So I won't hide them.

In my tears there is a cleansing
Each wound is washed until it's healed.
In my tears there is this hope
that what I believe really does exist,
even if I can't see it yet.

My tears are silent recognition
in moments when words are inadequate,
to give voice to what I feel.

So keep your tissue this time.
Let me cry.
These tears are mine.

Procrastination

I gotta stop dreamin'
so I can work on doin'.
Dreamin' without doin' ain't helpin' me none.
They ain't payin' no bills.
They ain't openin' no doors.
They are just there,
takin' up space
in my head,
slowin' down my day,
takin' my attention off doin' now.

I'm busy thinkin' 'bout what I might do tomorrow,
dreamin' 'bout
people I'll meet,
lives I'll change,
weight I'll lose,
money I'll make,
books I'll write,
places I'll see,
the woman I'll become someday.

I gotta stop dreamin'
so I can work on livin'
and do something different.

At least I'll get my butt out there and try.
Even if I fail,
I'm sure it'll be better than these dreams being stuck in my head
while my life passes me by.

You know, it's easier to just dream.
It takes much less effort
than writin' out plans,
settin' goals,
and holdin' myself accountable
for doin' what I said.

I gotta stop dreamin'
so I can work on bein'.
It takes more than dreams
to change those thoughts that won't let you sleep
from fantasy to reality.

In church they told me to speak of things I didn't see
as though they were already there.
But they never told me I was responsible
for doin' some of the work to make them appear.

I wonder how many others there are like me,
believin', just cuz you speak it, it's goin' to be.
But you gotta get outta the bed, son.
Get some stuff done.
Or you'll die wonderin'
where your dreams may have led,
if only you had gotten your procrastinatin' self outta bed.

Being

Born again with new vision
Endless possibilities ahead of me
I embrace what is new because I am
No longer bound by your definition of me.
God and I walk together, and I see me clearly.

Table Talk with Mom

I asked my mother what it was about my father that made her swoon.
She said, "Baby, everybody wanted to be with your father."
I nodded although I didn't understand that feeling.
See, I always assumed his love felt more like healthy teeth being pulled
without Novocain,
painful and unnecessary.

But I dare not tell her that I was mad at her for loving him.
So I sipped my tea
and smiled.

She poured her coffee
and talked about the life she lived before I lived.
Then it hit me.
She wasn't just my mother.
She was a woman,
caring and strong
who lived,
laughed,
made mistakes,
survived difficulties,
experienced joy,
dreamed,
loved,
and sacrificed for me.

And for a moment,
I was ashamed of myself
because I had judged her.
But she must have known what I was feeling,
so she hugged me tight
and said, "Loving your dad wasn't all that bad. After all, it's how I got you."

And a ritual that I never appreciated before, now had new meaning.
She gave me life, in that moment, at that table, in ways indescribable.
I needed it.
She knew it.
And she sipped her coffee
and smiled.

Dear Dad
(A Letter ... Kinda)

I'm sorry.
For years, I have wanted to live
while holding on to our old narrative,
the one from twenty-five years ago
when you weren't a very kind man.

I'm sorry for wanting to hold you frozen in time
while I grew and matured.
I preferred you in that box
because then I could talk about the woman I became
in spite of you.

Admittedly,
I am the woman I am,
in part, because of you.

And as much as I want to,
I don't know how to reconnect,
to remember us.
I don't know how to be me,
open and vulnerable with you.

Even now,
I feel like I am betraying myself by reaching out
while at the same time, I am missing out on love by holding back.
Why can't I escape the trauma of our past?

There's so much I need to say to you,
like "You hurt me to my core."
"How could you do it?"
I couldn't reconcile how you could be that man
and my father at the same time.

You were the man I stood against all my life.
You were the man in the background of every relationship,
reminding me not to love too much
because he might be just like you.

And I know you are different now.
I know you are.
I've seen it.
Some would say that your apology fifteen years ago was enough.

Maybe it was.
Maybe it is.

Perhaps it's time to acknowledge
that I'm the one who is frozen,
still that angry and scared girl,
worried that today is the day
you hurt me
and I am unable to recover.

I love you but give me some time.
I'm figuring out how to exist with you.
Fumbling through my words,
trying to figure out what to say to you,
I pause and I let my tears speak.

But instead of running away, this time, I sit with you,
fully present in this moment.
And I'll call this moment our beginning

His Love

Like a flood, his love
rose high,
washing away debris
others left behind.

Your Love
(A Haiku)

I can walk on clouds.
I can breathe underwater.
Your love be magic.

My Addiction

Sweet like candied yams with extra brown sugar,
I gorge until I'm satisfied.
You have that kind of loving
that will eventually cause my teeth to rot,
giving me cavities or something.
I know you're no good.
Still I cancel all my plans so my schedule is open,
just in case you happen to call.

Naked

We came together,
without hiding our flaws.
Intentionally removing our masks,
we presented our true selves.
There was no fear of being rejected.

We found joy
in not knowing what tomorrow would bring.
We found comfort in waking up each morning
wrapped in each others arms
learning to love,
determined to love.

Something special happens
when you are able to see yourself naked and still love.
Something magical happens
when you can see others naked and still love.
I want to experience that magic again.

She Knows

He said nothing,
but her name was etched on his heart.
And she could read well.

30

I want to love again.
But I'm too selfish to unwrap my heart
or share my time.

He Ain't Even Ready
(A Haiku)

Her love is ocean,
too deep for him to swim so
he just wet his feet.

Manipulation
(A Haiku)

Like piano keys,
she stroked his ego until
he played a new song.

Late-Night Thoughts
(I Remember You)

Baby, I remember you,
your touch,
the high I got from your scent,
your eyes,
the way you cupped my face in your hands the first time we kissed,
how you gently caressed my thighs the first time I stayed the night,
the tickle of your tongue on my neck and my back,
the way you held me tight.

You had that kind of loving that makes me lose track of time.
I couldn't help but think you were created with loving me in mind.
Once in a while, a song comes across my radio,
like tonight,
and my mind goes back to when it was
you
and me
together
loving each other.
And we did love each other.

Sometimes I wonder if I ever cross your mind.
And if I don't,
it's fine
but baby, I'm remembering you tonight.

35

Something in my spirit tells me
life is changing.
This burden is getting too heavy to carry.
Something is breaking, sometimes the breaking is painful.
I feel it.
When I close my eyes,
I see it.
And it's beautiful.
So I press on.

Street Cries
(A Haiku)

Her voice grew hoarse,
so the bloodstained concrete screamed out.
Another son lost.

Mama's Tears

Her tears flow nonstop.
They are as thick as blood.
Each of them contains a prayer.
God hears.

Righteous Rage

Have you ever noticed that the killing of black bodies is commonplace? I mean, have you noticed that there are systems designed to oppress everyone with a brown face?

I see traces of tears and fear on the faces of black mothers and anger and despair on the faces of her husband and her sons.

Her daughters cry out, "Where is justice?" And then she tries to block out the voice yelling back, "Black girl, for you there is none."

And after all these years, it's still the same old story.

It's horrific, brutal, and bloody.

This American story is so full of racism, hatred, and violence.

Politicians caution me to keep the peace when all they really want me to do is keep silent.

And that story they keep trying to sell me about equal opportunity, I just can't buy it.

They aren't the ones out here every day, trying to prove their life has value.

America, how many chokeholds will there be before the voice of Eric Garner haunts you? I can't breathe!

How many times will you stand your ground, killing another Trayvon Martin, guilty of carrying Skittles and iced tea?

How many Renisha McBrides will knock on a white man's door and get a shotgun to the head? How many Rekia Boyds, unarmed at the park will be shot dead?

How many Oscar Grants will be shot while facedown and hands cuffed behind his back?

How many Michael Browns, even after his death, will be viscously attacked?

How many Tarika Wilsons will be killed while holding their one-year-old son?

How many seven-year-old Aiyana Jones will be killed before her life has even begun?

Doesn't it seem like black and brown people are still disproportionately killed by the police?

I may not know all of their names, but I can still see the bloodstained concrete.

And, Mr. Officer, how can you be responsible to protect and serve the community,

when all that protecting and serving you're doing doesn't include me?

And then you look at Ferguson and wonder, Why the protest and the unrest?

But how long did you think you could step on necks of black people before they would fight back?

And don't for a moment think Ferguson is an anomaly.

No! Ferguson is Philly, Baltimore, Cleveland, Chicago, Detroit, and DC.

Is it me, or is 2014 looking more and more like 1960

with racism neatly woven into every system,

with disparities in education that leave entire communities poverty stricken,

with third-grade black boys and girls lined up to ride the pipeline to prison,

with police using excessive force as modern-day lynchings,

with unreasonable fear of black people because of the skin God put us in.

And sometimes I sit in my room wondering if God is really listening.

But I gotta believe that God hears and sees the cries and pleas of his people.

I gotta believe, when God created you and me, it wasn't for us to be less than but for us to be equal.

So while we're hoping and waiting for a godly disruption,

and while we're hoping and praying for our God to bring justice,

please don't throw up your hands in impotent frustration.

It's going to take more than saying, "Jesus, fix it!", to heal this nation.

So, Preachers, please come with more than that fiery talk. We need some solutions.

If you're just sitting in the pews while people die in the street, you will miss this revolution.

Bodies

Children's lives cut down like trees,
leaving mothers with wounds open,
bleeding.

Dear Preacher

I want you to know that this thing you've signed up for may sometimes bring you as much pain as it does joy. You'll have times when you smile, times when you cry and times when you just want to hide from the world. You'll find yourself spending more time in the street than you do in the pulpit. But God is there. You might find yourself preaching more in jails than you do in grand cathedrals. Just know God is there. You might feel like you are giving more than you have to give in order to feed hungry people who sometimes refuse to open their mouths. But know that God is there. And like the people to whom you'll preach, you might wrestle with anger, fear, depression, addiction, poverty and sickness. You'll want children and be unable to conceive. You'll wrestle with doubt, when you so desperately want to believe. You too will find yourself looking for a reason to hope in the midst of what seems like unanswered prayer. But Beloved, please know God is there. You'll have to speak a word of comfort even when God doesn't take away the pain. You'll have to speak about this new thing God is doing even when it seems everything remains the same. You'll even have to love on people when they've shown you they don't care. But Beloved, just know God is still there.

Untitled

Mother could no longer grieve.
Burying so many bodies can do that to you.
With eyes, now hollow,
and face, now sullen,
she could no longer smile.

All she could do was remember.
her dad warning her and her brothers about the evil things white folk in
the South did.
She learned quickly that they did evil things in the North too.

She remembered that her mom was scared as hell
when they decided to protest in the sixties.
She thought of the combination of biting pain and numbness she experienced
when they found her brother hanging from that tree.
The pain never left,
but she learned to live in spite of it.

She never thought she'd experience that kind of pain again.
Yet here it is.
And here she is,
trying to unravel the pain wrapped so tightly around her heart,
like the noose around her brother's throat.

Here she is,
learning to breathe again
in spite of the constant smell of death in the air.

Here she is,
wondering
if God is as powerful as they say.

She cries out,
How long, Lord?
And prays to remain steadfast during the silence.

Fire

I love to watch the fire breathe,
jump around,
dance,
and frantically move about.
almost as if trying to escape.

Consuming everything in its path,
Nothing—
and no one—
is safe.

It refuses to stop
until all is ruined.

39

The transformation to better
occurred over time.
I peeled away what was unnecessary.
Repaired what was broken as best I could,
picking up some joy and peace along the way
until I become whole
again.

Seasonal Friendship

Sisters,
held together
by a combination of cynicism
and hope.

Navigating waves of disappointment
in unison.

Believing though our journeys were different,
our destination was the same.

Time revealed it was not.

Who knew friendship was only a placeholder
to nourish you until you found love?

Living

You've never really lived
until the day you live shorn the opinions of others
and walk the path of your own truth.

But look at you now,
fighting to be you,
unapologetically living,
fearlessly loving,
and finally being
authentic and free.

40

Every wound,
every weakness,
every fear,
given over to God.

Rebuilt burned bridges.

From those I've wronged,
I asked forgiveness.

Finally admitted that I am not as together as they think.
No, I am not as together as I said.

But this year, I want to learn how to be generous with myself,
to remove the borders from my surrender,
the limits from my commitments.

I want to dive, eyes closed, into the water
without fear of drowning.
I want to leap
without worrying about where I land.

I want to risk something big
in order to do something good,
for myself,
for the world.

I want to see the beauty of each storm
and be refreshed by the rain.
Most importantly, I want to trust myself to love
and to be loved
again.

Printed in the United States
By Bookmasters